Exploring the Roots of Your Marriage

Understanding the Influence of the Family of Origin

Leticia S. Isidro-Clancy

STONEWALL PRESS
PAVING YOUR WAY TO SUCCESS

Printed in the United States of America

ISBN: Paperback: 978-1-948172-90-5
          eBook: 978-1-948172-89-9

Library of Congress Control Number:2018949023

STONEWALL PRESS
PAVING YOUR WAY TO SUCCESS

Stonewall Press
363 Paladium Court
Owings Mills, MD 21117
www.stonewallpress.com
1-888-334-0980

*This book is dedicated to the couples who are committed
to each other and strive to grow in their marriage.*

Contents

The commitment to complete this manual will have personal reward—
the discovery of oneself in the intimacy of the most important person
in your life, your spouse. This can lead to the growth of your marriage.

FOREWORD

Exploring the Roots of Your Marriage is a manual to promote the process of a growing marriage. This growth requires investigation of – and rediscovery of – the self through understanding ourselves in the context of our family of origin. As individual's awareness develops, the level of trust between partners will allow the risk of candid openness. As each couple progresses, they will realize that the positive and negative influences of the family of origin contribute to what happens in the marital relationship. This phenomenon is universal and generally unrecognized; in many cases it is the underlying cause when a marriage falters.

The purpose of examining our families of origin is not to blame our parents but to develop an understanding of what is behind the dynamics of our marriage and to effect change within us and in marriage. Without this awareness and acceptance, healing and becoming an integrated person is not possible.

The arrangement of topics is in progression and divided into four major segments: 1) reacquainting oneself with past experiences taken for granted as a justification for who we are, 2) rediscovering ourselves in the context of marriage 3) renewal of self by making changes to reinforce partnership in marriage, and 4) maintenance of marriage and prevention of the return to old behaviors.

This workbook allows motivated individuals in relationships to identify their issues with or without the help of a therapist. However, if in the process of working this program one or both partners find that there are personal issues interfering in their individual growth, and the growth of the marriage, it is highly recommended that they take responsibility to seek help from a professional. It takes honesty with oneself and motivation to admit this. It is possible that an individual may lose his/her objectivity in truly understanding the impact of their family of origin.

Any feedback or discussion from the spouse might be met with resistance and would fall on deaf ears. The loss of objectivity could be due to being entrenched in his/her family system. The individual perceives the dynamics of the family of origin as "being normal." Or, it could be due to a strong, and needed, denial system. If personal issues are not addressed prior or concomitant with the couple's work, the likelihood of achieving any change in the relationship will not happen. It is the prerogative of each person to change or not to change. Each one has the responsibility to make a choice to live or not in the "status quo" of the relationship. The choice may inevitably result in the termination of the marriage, but even deeper – in self-destructive decision-making.

This manual can serve as a therapist's guide in working with couples who struggle in understanding the impact of their family of origin on their relationship. *The best therapist cannot lead an individual unless that individual wishes to grow.

ACKNOWLEDGMENTS

To my parents Andres and Veronica Salo Isidro, who carried out their responsibilities as parents, and they taught me so many lessons in life and the importance of relationships.

To my six siblings, who epitomized the variations of self-development coming from one family. They taught me respect and acceptance of the differences in people.

To my husband, Marty, for his loving and continued support. He is also my most objective critics. He epitomizes the importance of a collaborating partner in our growing marriage.

To my children, Ligaya and Lee Martin, for their ever-continuing support, their loving presence in my life. They continue their manifest affirmation of who I am. Your living legacy is the value possible in all relationships.

My gratitude goes to the many couples that I have worked with both in the Retrouvaille Program and in my practice. Also, thank you, to couple friends, for sharing their experiences of their families of origin lessons, they validated observations.

To my friends, too many to name, who encouraged the pursuit of this book. To Karen Mullen, who was present in inception of this book, thank you for continued support. Most of all to Joanne Atwood, for her patience, creative thinking and organizational skills. And also for Jason's contribution in finalizing the production of this book with his computer expertise.

This manuscript would never have come into being without these pioneers in the work of the family of origin, Murray Bowen and Ivan

Bonzormenyi-Nagy, James L. Framo, and Susan Forward. Also, to Ronald Richardson for his *Family Ties that Bind*.

To the Office of Family Life, Diocese of Trenton, New Jersey, thank you for allowing me to share my work on families of origin with the many couples who participated in the Retrouville Program. My years of contact with them enriched my life.

PART 1

REACQUAINTING ONESELF
WITH PAST EXPERIENCES

HOW DID I BECOME ME?

HOW MY EXPERIENCES HAVE
IMPACTED WHO I AM?

How did I become me?

Negative experiences during the developmental process results in our perception that relationships are not safe.

In order to survive in an environment of rigid roles and rules, we adjust who we are and ignore our needs. The consequence is failure to develop the person we are meant to be.

It is difficult to admit to ourselves the truth about how much our parents may have hurt us as children and negatively impacted our lives. There are some of us who experienced early traumas in life that are painful and shameful. To protect ourselves from the pain we learned to build defenses. One of these defenses is to shut down or numb our feelings. If the feeling is triggered, we have subconsciously forgotten the origin.

How well do you know yourself?

What pain, shame, trauma, etc., have you experienced which resulted in destructive, dysfunctional, or self-defeating behavior?

What incidents or people helped bring about your self-awareness?

What behaviors result in distance rather than closeness in your relationships?

What feedback do you get about yourself?

Identify the areas in yourself you can work on (please check)

Inability to identify feelings/needs
Inability to trust others
Over controlling/ lack of control
Overly responsible/ irresponsible
Rigid/lacking boundaries
Distorted self image
Others (identify)

Positive traits that off-set your negative traits (please check)

Empathy
Understanding
Tolerance
Attentiveness
Patience
Perseverance
Openness
Kindness
Humor
Motivation
Determination
Inner Harmony
Others (identify)

Write notes to yourself of your insights, feelings and thoughts about your insights.

_____

_____

_____

_____

_____

_____

_____

_____

_____

_____

_____

_____

_____

_____

_____

_____

_____

_____

_____

_____

_____

_____

_____

Experiences as a young person

Check and circle what is applicable. If you experienced the opposite of what is listed below, please write it down.

Losses: divorce   death   separation   parent moving away

Neglect

Coldness

Overprotection

Hostility

Intrusiveness

Absent/ emotionally absent parent

Over/ under stimulation

Inconsistent/ insufficient control

Abuse: physical   emotional   sexual

Obsessive/compulsive behaviors: over cleanliness   alcoholism
                                 workaholism   food

Mental illness

Other (specify or explain)

Write notes to yourself of your insights, feelings and thoughts about your insights.

_____

_____

_____

_____

_____

_____

_____

_____

_____

_____

_____

_____

_____

_____

_____

_____

_____

_____

_____

_____

_____

_____

_____

Who am I?

The family tree (genogram) helps us understand how we became who we are. Learning about our family background gives us a sense of our own developmental process. The purpose of tracking how we came to be is not to put blame on our parents. The goal is to understand ourselves so we can take responsibility and make the necessary changes to enrich ourselves and our marriage. Looking at our family of origin will make us aware of the following:

> Understanding our developmental process will help us become aware of our negative traits. It is in the early stages of development that we learned the "how to's" in relationships: how to love, how to express our needs and the age-appropriate tasks.

> What we learned from our parents was what they learned from their own parents. Unless we make some changes, we will pass on the same legacy to our children.

Write notes to yourself of your insights, feelings and thoughts about your insights.

_____

_____

_____

_____

_____

_____

_____

_____

_____

_____

_____

_____

_____

_____

_____

_____

_____

_____

_____

_____

_____

_____

Significance of Terms

Boundary: Setting limit within oneself and between self and others.

Control: Inability to let go or to allow others to make responsibility for their thoughts and actions.

Emotional abuse: Behaviors that cause emotional suffering such as ignoring, verbal abuse, criticism.

Emotional disengagement: Being emotionally unaffected by another person.

Enabling: Being overly responsible for another person so that he/ she avoids self-responsibility.

Escapism: A tendency to ward off unpleasant feelings by addictive/ compulsive behavior, or by other avoidance maneuvers such as fantasizing, sleeping, overworking, overeating, etc.

Excessive guilt: Feeling guilty for things one is not responsible for. Feeling guilty to an inappropriate degree for a wrong doing.

Expression of feelings: Outwardly communicating one's feelings.

Family of origin: The group of people who played significant roles in your upbringing.

Identity: Your knowledge of yourself as a person and a sense of who you are that comes from within.

Impulsivity: Acting without understanding why or without evaluating the consequences of the action.

Intentional behavior: Conscious decision to behave in a certain way to achieve a desired result.

Intimacy: Mutual sharing of closeness (emotional, sexual, etc.)

Isolation: Lack of interpersonal connection with others.

Nuclear family: Make up of parents and children.

Openness: Being appropriately honest about one's feeling, willingness to respect other's feeling and point of view.

Physical abuse: Physically harmful actions: pushing hitting, choking, etc.

Responsible: Taking ownership for thoughts, feelings, action and accepting the consequences.

Role: The part you play in a relationship.

Sexual abuse: In appropriate sexual behavior. May be forced and may include touching, voyeurism, exhibiting sexual organ, etc. May be unforced (such as compliance by a child); any sexual behavior between an adult in apposition of authority or power and a child or person under their care.

Shame-based feeling: Perceiving and feeling "self" as being different, worthless and inadequate.

Genogram: Symbols and Meanings

A genogram is a way of mapping out your family tree. It will help you understand the legacy you have inherited from your parents and their parents. In tracking down the history of two generations, you will learn about their personal traits, behaviors, talents, preferences and family patterns. This journey will lead you to self-discovery. It will make you aware of the basis your uniqueness. You will learn that who you are and what you have become did not happen by accident. The strengths you have inherited from your parents, you may choose to cultivate. The limitations that you identify in yourself, even though it maybe rooted from two generations before you, can be changed to break the cycle of undesirable traits.

You have the chance to choose to be the best person you can be as an individual and in your marriage. The knowledge you gain from this process will also help you take responsibility for the legacy you pass on your own children.

The genogram allow you to trace multigenerational characteristics, conditioning and family traits – healthy and unhealthy – learned from grandparents. The goal is not to blame them but to take responsibility for your behavior and initiate change within yourself that will ultimately enrich your marriage.

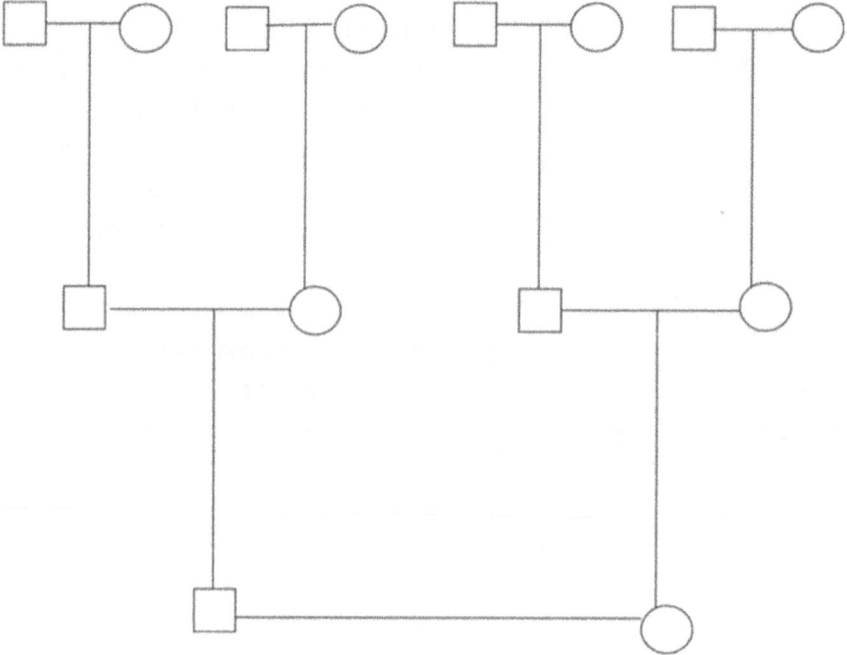

Male

Female

Deceased

Pregnancy

A Adopted

Marriage

Living Together Relationship

Divorce

Conflictual relationship

Very close relationship

Miscarriage

Children in birth order,
oldest → Youngest

Identical twins

Fraternal Twins

Divided Family

Conflicted Relationship
Parties involved do not get along
There is tension in the relationship.

Close Relationship
Healthy relationship – people involved are
caring and supportive of each other.

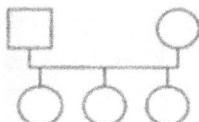

Very close relationship
Over involved – unhealthy relationship
characterized by being very dependent on each other.

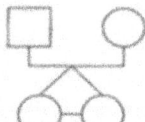

Distant Relationship
Lack of involvement between two people,
and avoidance of each other

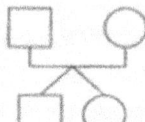

Cutoff Relationship
Two parties are estranged from each other due to
unresolved negative emotional attachment.
No contact but strong negative tie remains

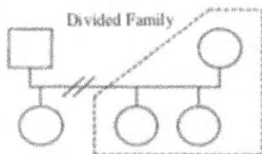

Adapted from the book *Genograms* by Emily Marlin

Guidelines in Working Your Genogram

As a child

- ☐ Did my parents fulfill or meet my needs?

- ☐ Did my parents make me feel "OK" or good about myself?

- ☐ Did I feel safe?

- ☐ Was I encouraged to express my thoughts and feelings?

- ☐ Did I have someone who believed in me, and/or listened to me?

- ☐ Was my family nurturing, trusting and validating?

- ☐ What behaviors did I see in my family that made me feel uncomfortable?

- ☐ What thoughts do I have about these behaviors?

- ☐ Did I learn to love, to trust, to listen and share?

The Influence of the Family of Origin

The family of origin affects three generations. Describe your relationship with each:

Your family of origin

Your present nuclear family

Your children's generation

Who am I?

Write notes to yourself of your insights, feelings and thoughts about your insights.

_____

_____

_____

_____

_____

_____

_____

_____

_____

_____

_____

_____

_____

_____

_____

_____

_____

_____

_____

_____

_____

_____

_____

_____

Continue to write as needed.

_____

_____

_____

_____

_____

_____

_____

_____

_____

_____

_____

_____

_____

_____

_____

_____

_____

_____

_____

_____

_____

- Reflect on what you have written
- Share key points with your spouse
- Hold on open dialogue with your spouse about you findings

Write notes to yourself of your insights, feelings and thoughts about your insights.

_____

_____

_____

_____

_____

_____

_____

_____

_____

_____

_____

_____

_____

_____

_____

_____

_____

_____

_____

_____

PART 2

═══

REDISCOVERING OURSELVES IN THE CONTEXT OF MARRIAGE

We become aware, or have a hint of the pain we unconsciously buried as a child, when we are confronted with it in close relationships as adults. This is particularly true in marriage. Often, when problems begin to surface, couples deal with it in a destructive way. We, unknowingly, sabotage the opportunity to develop a close relationship. It is in this context that our relationship skills are truly tested.

We bring to our marriage what we learned from our family of origin, and with it, certain expectations. When we experienced conflict in our marriage, we make an assessment: is it reality-based, or, is it the Family of Origin?

Take Your Marriage Pulse

We are products of our family of origin, conditioned to think, feel and respond in a specific way. Your relationship with your parents is reflected in your relationship with your spouse.

Gauge your emotional relationships with your parents from your present status as an adult. Agree or disagree with the following statements. Identify your thoughts and feelings. Write your thoughts and feeling how they influence your relationship with your spouse.

My parents do not recognize me as an adult.	I do not feel comfortable accepting gift from my parents.
I am not able to hold my own when I am with my parents.	I avoid long visits with my parents.

My parents' gifts, monetary or otherwise, come with 'string attached'

The opinions of my parents influence my major decisions.

I have strong emotional reactions when I hear myself sounding like my mother/father

My parents' negative remarks outweigh their positive ones.

I have strong reactions to criticism from my parents..

My parents have an impact on my style of handling conflicts with my spouse.

I shut down to avoid conflict
with my parents.

I purposely try to be different
from my parents.

My parents control me (or will controll me) even from the grave!

I wish to change (some, most all) of the above.

Name: _____   Date: _____

SELF-DISCOVERY IN MARRIAGE

Self-discovery comes about when we are willing to take the risk of being intimately known by our spouse. Our experience of self-validation from our family of origin correlates with our level of self-acceptance and self-confidence. This influence how open we are in entrusting our most inner being to another person, believing that it will be honored. Consequently, we are predisposed to a certain level of intimacy. Intimacy means communicating one's goodness and being appreciated by the other.

How Healthy Is Your Marriage?

A static marriage is not healthy.

A marriage in <u>crisis</u> can be a healthy sign

➢ The partnership is not content with the status quo of the relationship

➢ Changes are required to heal the marriage

➢ Each partner plays a vital role in making the changes. The efforts of one person alone cannot improve a marriage.

RELATIONSHIPS SKILLS

Rank (1 = low, 5 = high) each area. Mark family of origin. O- mother ☐ - father

	Family of Origin					Spouse					Self				
Self-Management															
Self-talk	1	2	3	4	5	1	2	3	4	5	1	2	3	4	5
Self-understanding	1	2	3	4	5	1	2	3	4	5	1	2	3	4	5
Self-care	1	2	3	4	5	1	2	3	4	5	1	2	3	4	5
Self-esteem	1	2	3	4	5	1	2	3	4	5	1	2	3	4	5
Relationships															
Intra-personal	1	2	3	4	5	1	2	3	4	5	1	2	3	4	5
Inter-personal	1	2	3	4	5	1	2	3	4	5	1	2	3	4	5
Family	1	2	3	4	5	1	2	3	4	5	1	2	3	4	5
Friends	1	2	3	4	5	1	2	3	4	5	1	2	3	4	5
Feelings															
Understanding	1	2	3	4	5	1	2	3	4	5	1	2	3	4	5
Expressive	1	2	3	4	5	1	2	3	4	5	1	2	3	4	5
Connecting feelings & behavior	1	2	3	4	5	1	2	3	4	5	1	2	3	4	5
Communication															
Distancing	1	2	3	4	5	1	2	3	4	5	1	2	3	4	5
Connecting	1	2	3	4	5	1	2	3	4	5	1	2	3	4	5
Styles															
Assertive	1	2	3	4	5	1	2	3	4	5	1	2	3	4	5
Aggressive	1	2	3	4	5	1	2	3	4	5	1	2	3	4	5
Passive	1	2	3	4	5	1	2	3	4	5	1	2	3	4	5
Passive/ Aggressive	1	2	3	4	5	1	2	3	4	5	1	2	3	4	5
Listening															
Active	1	2	3	4	5	1	2	3	4	5	1	2	3	4	5
Feedback	1	2	3	4	5	1	2	3	4	5	1	2	3	4	5
Giving	1	2	3	4	5	1	2	3	4	5	1	2	3	4	5
Receiving	1	2	3	4	5	1	2	3	4	5	1	2	3	4	5

FRAMEWORK OF RELATIONSHIPS

Rank (1 = low, 5 = high) each area. Mark family of origin. O- mother ☐ - father

Relationships	Family of Origin					Spouse					Self				
Intimacy	1	2	3	4	5	1	2	3	4	5	1	2	3	4	5
Openness	1	2	3	4	5	1	2	3	4	5	1	2	3	4	5
Expression of Feelings	1	2	3	4	5	1	2	3	4	5	1	2	3	4	5
Emotional Engagement	1	2	3	4	5	1	2	3	4	5	1	2	3	4	5
Responsibility															
Enabling	1	2	3	4	5	1	2	3	4	5	1	2	3	4	5
Control	1	2	3	4	5	1	2	3	4	5	1	2	3	4	5
Reality Orientation															
Impulsivity	1	2	3	4	5	1	2	3	4	5	1	2	3	4	5
Isolation	1	2	3	4	5	1	2	3	4	5	1	2	3	4	5
Shame	1	2	3	4	5	1	2	3	4	5	1	2	3	4	5
Guilt	1	2	3	4	5	1	2	3	4	5	1	2	3	4	5
Escapism															
Substance Abuse	1	2	3	4	5	1	2	3	4	5	1	2	3	4	5
Workaholism	1	2	3	4	5	1	2	3	4	5	1	2	3	4	5
Gambling	1	2	3	4	5	1	2	3	4	5	1	2	3	4	5
Sex	1	2	3	4	5	1	2	3	4	5	1	2	3	4	5
Other	1	2	3	4	5	1	2	3	4	5	1	2	3	4	5
Abuse	1	2	3	4	5	1	2	3	4	5	1	2	3	4	5
Physical	1	2	3	4	5	1	2	3	4	5	1	2	3	4	5
Emotional	1	2	3	4	5	1	2	3	4	5	1	2	3	4	5
Sexual	1	2	3	4	5	1	2	3	4	5	1	2	3	4	5
Commitment															
Motivation	1	2	3	4	5	1	2	3	4	5	1	2	3	4	5
Determination	1	2	3	4	5	1	2	3	4	5	1	2	3	4	5
Inner Harmony	1	2	3	4	5	1	2	3	4	5	1	2	3	4	5

ELEMENTS OF LOVING RELATIONSHIP: COMMITMENT, PASSION, AND INTIMACY

Rate yourself, your spouse and your family of origini with a + or − in each box

THE ELEMENTS	SELF	SPOUSE	MOTHER	FATHER
COMMITMENT - promise of exclusivity				
Sees good in the relationship				
Values the investment in the relationship				
Values the identity as a couple				
Awareness that each contributes to the problem				
INTIMACY - closeness, emotional value				
Sees good in self & spouse				
Affirms the value of the other person				
Appreciates the other person's actions				
Affection is shown verbally and physically				
CARING - concern with one another's welfare				
Trustworthy				
Reliable				
PROTECTIVE - maintain integrity as a couple				
Spending time as a couple				
ENJOYMENT - as individuals & as a couple				
Negotiate activities that are pleasurable				
Initiate enjoyable activities				
RESPONSIBILITY - accepts share of problem				
Accepts interdependence in the relationship				
Does not blame others				
SHARING HURT- in order to find a solution				
Recognizes that anger masks other feelings				
Looks at pattern of hurtful behavior				
Examines the source of hurtful behavior				
FORGIVENESS- Acceptance & understanding				
Validates hurt in self and partner				
Recognizes unforgiven hurts = resentment				
PASSION - Affection, longing, sex				
Share likes and dislikes				
Spontaneous				

Write notes to yourself of your insights, feelings and thoughts about your insights.

_____

_____

_____

_____

_____

_____

_____

_____

_____

_____

_____

_____

_____

_____

_____

_____

_____

_____

_____

_____

_____

_____

_____

_____

Sound marriages have things in common

Each troubled marriage has issues unique to itself

As adults we might be cognitively aware of
the changes we need to make to sustain
a mature, nurturing relationship.
However, the fragmentation
of our childhood makes it
difficult to share what
we are not sure we
have-

OURSELVES.

We look to our spouse
to fill the needs we missed
in our childhood, unaware that
our spouse is in the same boat as we are.

THE 3 R's OF MARRIAGE
ISSUE THEMES:

REALITY ORIENTATION

RESPONSIBILITY

RELATIONSHIP

REALITY ORIENTATION:

Are you grounded in the here and now? Are you in tune with the present? Failure to focus on the present is the result of your experiences within your *Family of Origin*.

DO YOU UNDERSTAND YOURSELF WITHIN YOUR MARRIAGE?

Are my expectations grounded in reality, OR, are they based on my Family of Origin?

Are my present needs and desires influenced by unmet needs from my youth?

Are my emotional expectations 'normal,' OR, are they from my *Family of Origin?*

Identify your behaviors when REALITY-BASED thinking is lacking:

✓ Impulsive

✓ Shame or guilt

✓ Isolation

✓ Poor self worth

✓ Escapism – Addiction – Compulsive

✓ Abusive – physical, verbal, emotional or sexual

✓ Type A - workaholic

RESPONSIBILITY:

The ability to be an equal partner in all aspects of a marital relationship

YOUR SENSE OF RESPONSIBILITY

What was my childhood role? How did it contribute to the stability of my family or origin?

As a youth, were you given responsibilities for yourself/others?

What responsibilities in my youth were age-appropriate?

If not, did your parents ENABLED you to be a child throughout your life

How did my youthful responsibilities define me as an adult person?

Who influenced my adult attitude toward responsibility?	How does this apply to my sense of responsibility in marriage?

What behaviors demonstrate my effort (or lack of effort) to take responsibility in my marriage?	How does my sense of responsibility provide direction to the life of my family?

WHAT IS YOUR SHARE IN EACH OF THE FOLLOWING?

Explore with your spouse your understanding of the areas of concern and your willingness to participate in these areas.

Finances	Decision-making

Self care	Household chores

Parenting and child care	Emotional availability

FAILURE TO SHARE WILL AFFECT YOUR MARRIAGE

RELATIONSHIPS:

An individual's relationships are grounded in their Reality Orientation, or its lack.

SELF-ASSESSMENT

Are my responses to my spouse (or any situation) a replica of my father's mother's actions/words?	What feelings/behaviors, acceptable in your *Family of Origin*, are causing problems in your present relationship?
What gets in the way of understanding my spouse's point of view when we are in conflict?	When in conflict with my spouse, what stops me from compromising on an issue?
What do I look for from my spouse to confirm that I am loved and valued?	What is the most important goal in resolving conflicts with my spouse?

YOU AND MARRIAGE

How willing are you to participate in these areas of your marriage?
Score yourself from 1 to 7 with seven the highest possible.

+ Intimacy   1   2   3   4   5   6   7
+ Openness   1   2   3   4   5   6   7
+ Expression of feeling   1   2   3   4   5   6   7
+ Emotional engagement   1   2   3   4   5   6   7

WITH YOUR SPOUSE, EXPLORE YOUR UNDERSTANDING OF THESE AREAS AND YOUR WILLINGNESS TO PARTICIPATE IN EACH. BE OPEN TO A DIALOGUE.

Sexuality In Marriage

Human beings are meant to bond together. Apart from the bond between a parent and a child, there is no other bond stronger than the bond in marriage. In marriage we make the vow for life. However, in many cases, couples drift apart and become emotionally disconnected. Some couples maintain the façade of closeness as the publicly carry out their roles routinely as husband and wife and as parents. Privately the feeling of not being emotionally connected with each other is felt in their lack of intimacy, specifically in the areas of communication and their sexual relationship.

Strong bonds do not happen spontaneously and naturally. It takes intentionality, a conscious decision to act in a certain way to achieve a needed result. The responsibility to make the bond strong lies on bother partners, in the belief that their marriage is important.

Write notes to yourself of your insights, feelings and thoughts about your insights.

_____

_____

_____

_____

_____

_____

_____

_____

_____

_____

_____

_____

_____

_____

_____

_____

_____

_____

_____

_____

_____

Keep in mind that many of your beliefs, feelings and behaviors are learned from your family origin. There are messages learned early in life that are related to sexuality and that have become part of your outlook in life.

The following questions will help you examine how this outlook is operational in your relationship with your spouse.

1. How comfortable are you in initiating physical intimacy with your spouse?

2. What thoughts and feelings do you have when you initiate sex with your spouse?

3. What circumstances or setting do you find uncomfortable in being intimate with your spouse?

4. How comfortable are you saying "no" to your spouse when he/she initiates sex?

5. What are the differences between you and your spouse when it comes to your needs for physical intimacy? Frequency? Physical expression?

6. What role does touching play in the expression of your physical intimacy toward each other?

7. How aware are you of the positive or negative changes within yourself during sex with your spouse?

Write notes to yourself of your insights, feelings and thoughts about your insights.

_____

_____

_____

_____

_____

_____

_____

_____

_____

_____

_____

_____

_____

_____

_____

_____

_____

_____

_____

_____

_____

_____

_____

_____

1. On the scale of 1 to 5 (high) how often do you use sex:

    _____ as a way of getting what you want from your spouse?

    _____ as a way creating distance between you and your spouse?

    _____ as a way of creating closeness?

2. How would you like your spouse to demonstrate to you physically that s/he loves you?

3. What difficulties are you experiencing in your sexual relationship with your spouse?

4. How do you feel talking about sex with your spouse?

5. How do you feel about your own sexuality? About sex itself?

6. As a result of you awareness, what specific changes are you willing to make to improve your sexual relationship with your spouse?

7. Share and explore with your spouse your insight and understanding of your own sexuality.

Write notes to yourself of your insights, feelings and thoughts about your insights.

_____

_____

_____

_____

_____

_____

_____

_____

_____

_____

_____

_____

_____

_____

_____

_____

_____

_____

_____

_____

_____

_____

_____

_____

PART 3

RENEWAL OF SELF BY MAKING
CHANGES TO REINFORCE
PARTNERSHIP IN MARRIAGE

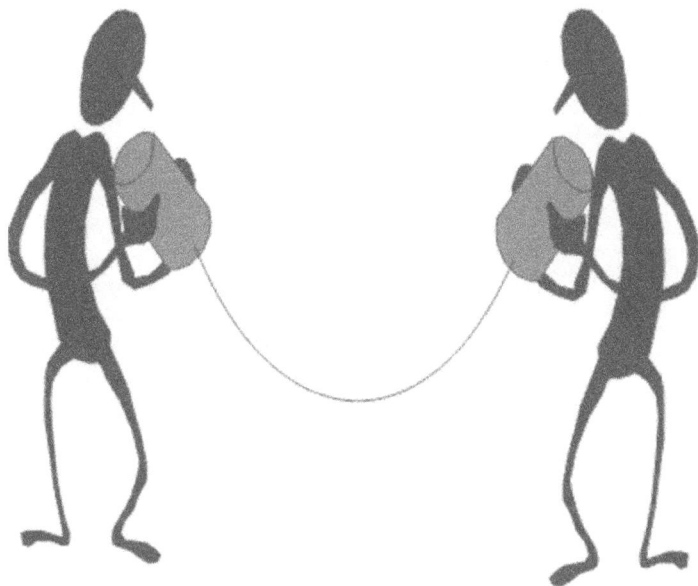

How Do We Mend Our Marriage?

It takes two healthy, emotionally secure people to have a healthy relationship. Many of us look to our spouse to make us feel complete and wonderful. When this fails, to maintain some equilibrium in marriage, we learned to cope. Once again, we adjust who we are until it becomes intolerable, and we start drifting away from each other.

Differences and conflicts between two people are inevitable, a reality that we need to accept. It is not necessary to lose and sacrifice who we are to save our marriage. Both individuals need to recognize their contribution in making the marriage a growing experience. It is a deliberate and an intentional process. Love is a decision.

THE HEALING PROCESS

HEALING a marriage is based upon the following premises

- As a spouse, I will define my role in the success or failure of this marriage.

  > What role have you assumed?
  >
  >
  > How does it help or hinder the marriage?

- Marriage is not a competition it is a partnership.

  > What strengths do I bring into this marriage to compliment my partner's strengths?

- Trust is the capital investment in marriage.

  > How much do I trust myself to work on this marriage?
  >
  >
  > How much do I trust my spouse to work on this marriage?

• As a spouse I have the responsibility to monitor myself

Self-monitoring check list:

➤ What words/phrases do I consistently use to express myself?

➤ What message is relayed by my body language/facial expression?

➤ What is the tone of my voice?

➤ Do I just listen, or do I really HEAR what my spouse has to say?

➤ Do I feel vulnerable when I talk about my feelings or myself?

➤ What words or actions trigger reactions in me?

➤ What are the thoughts and feelings behind these reactions?

➤ Are these thoughts, feelings, reactions reality-based or from my Family of Origin?

- As a spouse I need to identify and change behaviors that gratify my needs at the expense of the marriage

> List specific behaviors that cause conflict between you and your spouse

> Discuss the identified behaviors, prioritize and agree upon a starting point. SEE PAGE 5

> Agree on the support methods your spouse will provide

> Implement new actions; 'Act as if"

I need to demonstrate sensitivity towards my spouse by:

- Expressing my perceptions of the feelings and concerns of my spouse.

- Sharing recognition of verbal and non-verbal feelings, needs and concerns of my spouse.

- Anticipating the emotional effects of specific behaviors and sharing them with my spouse.

- Re-stating my understanding of my spouse's point of view and asking for feedback for accuracy.

HOLD A DIALOGUE WITH YOUR SPOUSE SHARING INTERNAL CONFLICTS AND DISCOMFORTS. EXPECT FEEDBACK.

RELATIONSHIP MAINTENANCE

The 4 Fs of Maintaining Your Marriage – how do you express the following behaviorally?

Being FAITHFUL

> means - believing in the importance of your marriage - recognizing and accepting the demands of marriage

Being FORGIVING

> means – accepting the hurt, the feeling of being wronged and letting go of the resentment

Being FLEXIBLE

> means – acceptance of the changes in marriage
> - supportive of the spouse's development
> - accommodating the needs of others such as the children

Being FUN

> means - the willingness to make an investment in creating enjoyment in relationship.
> Free time
> Companionship
> Agreed mutual interest

Write notes to yourself of your insights, feelings and thoughts about your insights.

_____

_____

_____

_____

_____

_____

_____

_____

_____

_____

_____

_____

_____

_____

_____

_____

_____

_____

_____

_____

_____

_____

_____

_____

Keeping The Commitment Alive

IDENTIFY your part in the equation

Set and maintain BOUNDARIES

Set aside TIME TO BE TOGETHER; keep the relationship alive

Jointly DECIDE the first step in improving your marriage

Above all, COMMUNICATE!

INITIATE dialogue

SELF-DISCLOSE voluntarily

SHARE insights, pain, self-discovery

Write notes to yourself of your insights, feelings and thoughts about your insights.

_____

_____

_____

_____

_____

_____

_____

_____

_____

_____

_____

_____

_____

_____

_____

_____

_____

_____

_____

_____

_____

_____

_____

_____

RESOLVE ISSUES BEFORE THEY BECOME CHRONIC OR A CRISIS

Sensitizing yourself to the subtlety of self-deception is an important way of ensuring that you will not slip back to behavioral patterns that will sabotage the work that you have done so far toward strengthening your marriage. Awareness and insights you have developed are valuable in an on-going evaluation of how you want your marriage to be.

ISSUES AND CONFLICT RESOLUTION

DEFINE THE PROBLEM

☐ Set aside your issue, your anger, your "ego" and
    ☐ LISTEN to the words, the tone and the meaning of your spouse.

☐ Focus on the current issue
    - "You're doing it again... you always...."
    + "I'm really upset over what you are doing/saying. Please explain it to me so I can understand."

☐ Clarify
    + "I hear you saying......"

CONFLICT RESOLUTION SKILLS

☐ Take responsibility for yourself without blaming
    + "I feel ......"
    - "You make me....."

☐ Avoid crossing over (Talk about you. Ask about your spouse)
    - "You need to look at ...."
    + "I need help, how can we work on this?"

☐ Practice active listening; paraphrase.
    + "I want to understand, are you saying ..."

    ☐ Make every effort to understand your partner without being judgmental

Write notes to yourself of your insights, feelings and thoughts about your insights.

_____

_____

_____

_____

_____

_____

_____

_____

_____

_____

_____

_____

_____

_____

_____

_____

_____

_____

_____

_____

_____

DIFFUSE POTENTIALLY TOXIC SITUATIONS

❖ **DISENGAGE** when a conflict threatens to escalate to a destructive level.

> **AGREE** on a time to re-engage

❖ **TAKE** responsibility for self-soothing

❖ **RE-E NGAGE** when both parties are calm

> **RESTATE** the initial positions

> **EXPLORE** underlying concerns

> **PURSUE** creative solutions that address concerns

Write notes to yourself of your insights, feelings and thoughts about your insights.

_____

_____

_____

_____

_____

_____

_____

_____

_____

_____

_____

_____

_____

_____

_____

_____

_____

_____

_____

_____

_____

_____

PART 4

Marriage and Prevention of the
Return to Old Behaviors

PREVENT THE CYCLE

Marriages fail when we give up due to frustration of repeated setbacks and the appearance that nothing will change. It is easy to forget the many years of buried pains and confusion that made us estrange even to ourselves. We have to be alert to our own signals of relapse and how tempting it is to go back to the familiar pattern of behaviors that could lead us back to the road of isolation and disconnectedness. To prevent the cycle, we strengthen our commitment by "acting as if" until the new behavior is internalized. The experience becomes self-rewarding. This is due to the realization of self-empowerment, the feeling that "I can do it," which is being reinforced by the positive response we received from our spouse.

OOPS, I DID IT AGAIN!

Emotional Relapse: Going back to familiar habits even though you are aware of the negative consequences.

- ◆ Why is it difficult to stay on track?

- ◆ What is behind my resistance to change?

- ◆ What experiences from my family of origin blocks my growth in this marriage?

- ◆ Am I willing to continue the process of change?

SELF-MONITORING FOR WARNING SIGNALS OF RELAPSE

- gradual drifting into my old patterns

- insensitivity to my spouse's concerns

- unwillingness to evaluate my thinking and feeling in relation to my behavior

- my personal needs placed in higher priority over the need of marriage

- omitting important self-disclosure with my spouse

DEALING WITH A RELAPSE

Accept, Forgive, and Continue to Love, then:

- Self-examine

- Disclose

- Communicate openly

- Hear and listen

- Receive feedback

SPIRITUALITY IN MARRIAGE

Recognizing that the two people in marriage come from different backgrounds, there is bound to be conflicts that need to be worked out. Prolonged and chronic issues could make the partners question their ability to continue their commitment to the marriage. For many of us, our beliefs help in maintaining our commitment. Reflect on the following questions:

- During difficult times, what beliefs help me sustain my commitment to my marriage?

- How do my personal beliefs impact my own growth in the context of my marriage?

- What influence do my own beliefs and my spouse's beliefs have on our marriage?

- How does the rhythm of the ebb and flow of my inner harmony impact my marriage?

- For myself and my spouse, what is the role of forgiveness and acceptance in the strength of our marriage?

- How do my spouse's beliefs (or lack of) affect my marriage?

- What gives me hope to continue my commitment to my marriage?

Write notes to yourself of your insights, feelings and thoughts about your insights.

_____

_____

_____

_____

_____

_____

_____

_____

_____

_____

_____

_____

_____

_____

_____

_____

_____

_____

_____

_____

_____

_____

_____

_____

LOVING, FORGIVING, AND ACCEPTING

The success and failure of my marriage depends on forgiving my spouse and myself for the disappointments I experience in our marriage. I recognize my share in the responsibility for making the marriage work, and that I am willing to collaborate in this effort. I make a deliberate decision to continue to love each other.

I affirm the above statement.

Name: _____

Date: _____

Your journey in exploring the roots of your marriage leads you to rediscover who you are in the intimacy of the most important person in your life, your spouse, and it leads you to your growth together in marriage.

SUGGESTED READINGS

Barker, P. Basic family therapy. New York: Oxford University International Press, 1986.

Boss, E. & Davis, L. The Courage to Heal. New York: Harper and Row Publishers, 1988.

Bradshaw, J. Healing The Shame That Binds You. Deerfield Beach: Health Communications, Inc., 1988.

Forward, S. Emotional Blackmail. Deerfield Beach: Harper Collins Publishers, Inc., 1997.

Forward, S. Toxic Parents. New York: Bantam Books, 1989.

Framo, J. L. Family of Origin Therapy. New York: Bruner/Mazel Inc., 1992.

Gottman, J., Notarius, C., Gonso, J. & Markman, H. A Couple's Guide To Communication. Champaign, Illinois: Research Press, 1976.

Kurtz, E. Shame And Guilt. Hazelden, 1976.

Lobsennz, N. & Weinsinger, H. Nobody's Perfect. Los Angeles: Stratford Press, 1981.

Marlin, E. Genograms. Chicago: Contemporary Books, 1989.

Miller, A. For Your Own Good. New York: Farrar, Straus, Giroux, 1983.

Paine-Gernee, K. & Hunt, T. Emotional Healing. New York: Warner Books, Inc., 1990.

Richardson, R. Family Ties That Bind. Canada: International Self Counsel Press, 1984.

Whitfiled, C. A Gift To Myself. Deerfield Beach: Health Communications Inc., 1990.

Woititz, J.G. Adult Children Of Alcoholics. Pompani Beach: Health Communications Inc., 1983.

APPENDICES

Post Tests

- RELATIONSHIPS SKILLS
- FRAMEWORK OF RELATIONSHIPS
- ELEMENTS OF LOVING RELATIONSHIP:
  COMMITMENT, PASSION, AND INTIMACY
- INTERVIEW QUESTIONS

RELATIONSHIPS SKILLS

Rank (1 = low, 5 = high) each area. Mark family of origin. O- mother   ☐ - father

	Family of Origin	Spouse	Self
Self-Management			
Self-talk	1 2 3 4 5	1 2 3 4 5	1 2 3 4 5
Self-understanding	1 2 3 4 5	1 2 3 4 5	1 2 3 4 5
Self-care	1 2 3 4 5	1 2 3 4 5	1 2 3 4 5
Self-esteem	1 2 3 4 5	1 2 3 4 5	1 2 3 4 5
Relationships			
Intra-personal	1 2 3 4 5	1 2 3 4 5	1 2 3 4 5
Inter-personal	1 2 3 4 5	1 2 3 4 5	1 2 3 4 5
Family	1 2 3 4 5	1 2 3 4 5	1 2 3 4 5
Friends	1 2 3 4 5	1 2 3 4 5	1 2 3 4 5
Feelings			
Understanding	1 2 3 4 5	1 2 3 4 5	1 2 3 4 5
Expressive	1 2 3 4 5	1 2 3 4 5	1 2 3 4 5
Connecting feelings & behavior	1 2 3 4 5	1 2 3 4 5	1 2 3 4 5
Communication			
Distancing	1 2 3 4 5	1 2 3 4 5	1 2 3 4 5
Connecting	1 2 3 4 5	1 2 3 4 5	1 2 3 4 5
Styles			
Assertive	1 2 3 4 5	1 2 3 4 5	1 2 3 4 5
Aggressive	1 2 3 4 5	1 2 3 4 5	1 2 3 4 5
Passive	1 2 3 4 5	1 2 3 4 5	1 2 3 4 5
Passive/ Aggressive	1 2 3 4 5	1 2 3 4 5	1 2 3 4 5
Listening			
Active	1 2 3 4 5	1 2 3 4 5	1 2 3 4 5
Feedback	1 2 3 4 5	1 2 3 4 5	1 2 3 4 5
Giving	1 2 3 4 5	1 2 3 4 5	1 2 3 4 5
Receiving	1 2 3 4 5	1 2 3 4 5	1 2 3 4 5

FRAMEWORK OF RELATIONSHIPS

Rank (1 = low, 5 = high) each area. Mark family of origin. O- mother ☐ - father

	Family of Origin					Spouse					Self				
Relationships															
Intimacy	1	2	3	4	5	1	2	3	4	5	1	2	3	4	5
Openness	1	2	3	4	5	1	2	3	4	5	1	2	3	4	5
Expression of Feelings	1	2	3	4	5	1	2	3	4	5	1	2	3	4	5
Emotional Engagement	1	2	3	4	5	1	2	3	4	5	1	2	3	4	5
Responsibility															
Enabling	1	2	3	4	5	1	2	3	4	5	1	2	3	4	5
Control	1	2	3	4	5	1	2	3	4	5	1	2	3	4	5
Reality Orientation															
Impulsivity	1	2	3	4	5	1	2	3	4	5	1	2	3	4	5
Isolation	1	2	3	4	5	1	2	3	4	5	1	2	3	4	5
Shame	1	2	3	4	5	1	2	3	4	5	1	2	3	4	5
Guilt	1	2	3	4	5	1	2	3	4	5	1	2	3	4	5
Escapism															
Substance Abuse	1	2	3	4	5	1	2	3	4	5	1	2	3	4	5
Workaholism	1	2	3	4	5	1	2	3	4	5	1	2	3	4	5
Gambling	1	2	3	4	5	1	2	3	4	5	1	2	3	4	5
Sex	1	2	3	4	5	1	2	3	4	5	1	2	3	4	5
Other	1	2	3	4	5	1	2	3	4	5	1	2	3	4	5
Abuse	1	2	3	4	5	1	2	3	4	5	1	2	3	4	5
Physical	1	2	3	4	5	1	2	3	4	5	1	2	3	4	5
Emotional	1	2	3	4	5	1	2	3	4	5	1	2	3	4	5
Sexual	1	2	3	4	5	1	2	3	4	5	1	2	3	4	5
Commitment															
Motivation	1	2	3	4	5	1	2	3	4	5	1	2	3	4	5
Determination	1	2	3	4	5	1	2	3	4	5	1	2	3	4	5
Inner Harmony	1	2	3	4	5	1	2	3	4	5	1	2	3	4	5

ELEMENTS OF LOVING RELATIONSHIP: COMMITMENT, PASSION, AND INTIMACY

Rate yourself, your spouse and your family of origini with a + or − in each box

THE ELEMENTS	SELF	SPOUSE	MOTHER	FATHER
COMMITMENT - promise of exclusivity				
Sees good in the relationship				
Values the investment in the relationship				
Values the identity as a couple				
Awareness that each contributes to the problem				
INTIMACY - closeness, emotional value				
Sees good in self & spouse				
Affirms the value of the other person				
Appreciates the other person's actions				
Affection is shown verbally and physically				
CARING - concern with one another's welfare				
Trustworthy				
Reliable				
PROTECTIVE - maintain integrity as a couple				
Spending time as a couple				
ENJOYMENT - as individuals & as a couple				
Negotiate activities that are pleasurable				
Initiate enjoyable activities				
RESPONSIBILITY - accepts share of problem				
Accepts interdependence in the relationship				
Does not blame others				
SHARING HURT - in order to find a solution				
Recognizes that anger masks other feelings				
Looks at pattern of hurtful behavior				
Examines the source of hurtful behavior				
FORGIVENESS- Acceptance & understanding				
Validates hurt in self and partner				
Recognizes unforgiven hurts = resentment				
PASSION - Affection, longing, sex				
Share likes and dislikes				
Spontaneous				

INTERVIEW QUESTIONS

1. Describe how this manual has helped you and your marriage?

2. Assuming that you have gained some understanding of yourself through this manual, how willing are you to take the risk in disclosing your thoughts and feelings to your spouse?

3. In examining your family of origin, what did you discover that is significant in your understanding of the dynamics of your relationship with your spouse?

4. What specific changes in yourself and in your marriage are you working on, as a result of your involvement in the workshop and on the work you have done using the manual *Exploring the Roots of Your Marriage?*

5. What areas in your marriage do you feel you have gained a better understanding of, as a result of working on this manual?

6. What role did the charts on the "Relationship Skills," "Framework Relationships" and "Elements of Loving Relationship" play in identifying and understanding the influences of your family of origin on:
    a. the positive aspects of your marriage?
    b. negative aspects of your marriage?

www.ingramcontent.com/pod-product-compliance
Lightning Source LLC
Chambersburg PA
CBHW031131020426
42333CB00012B/333